What Your Sales Managers Never Teach You

What Your Sales Managers Never Teach You

Eleven Secrets to Sales Success

Kevin Foo

PARTRIDGE

To order additional copies of this book, contact
Toll Free 800 101 2657 (Singapore)
Toll Free 1 800 81 7340 (Malaysia)
orders.singapore@partridgepublishing.com

www.partridgepublishing.com/singapore

Contents

Introduction: Reflections on a Mediocre Career 11

Chapter 1: The Eight Rules of Engagement 13

Chapter 2: Waking from the Sleepwalk 15

Chapter 3: The Student Becomes the Teacher 21

Chapter 4: Lesson 1: Don't Ask How; Ask Why 25

Chapter 5: Lesson 2: When You Lose, Don't Lose the Lesson 33

Chapter 6: Lesson 3: The Deal Before the Deal 37

Chapter 7: Lesson 4: Back to Better Basics 42

Chapter 8: Lesson 5: The Million-Dollar Deal 52

Chapter 9: Lesson 6: Mirror 57

Chapter 10: Lesson 7: Harness the Power of Persuasion 60

Chapter 11: Lesson 8: First sell problems, then sell solutions 67

Chapter 12: Lesson 9: Be Yourself 72

Chapter 13: Lesson 10: Suspect or Prospect 77

Chapter 14: Lesson 11: Invest in Yourself 81

Chapter 15: Reap the Rewards 84

Summary 87

Dedication

To my beloved wife, Ashley Thng, who has endured the hard journey with me. Success didn't come easy – the initial journey was tough and poor – yet she has always seen the potential in me.

Acknowledgements

Tribute to my wife, my mentors, friends, key people in the financial industry who have helped me in providing inputs, as well as colleagues all of whom have graciously shared their experiences and ideas with me.

Introduction

Reflections on a Mediocre Career

Selling has always been and will forever be a lucrative career, but for many professional salespeople, it's a perpetual struggle. In your heart, you know you can do more and earn more, but you're not sure what path to take. How do you get from where you are now to where you want to be?

I've been there.

For twelve years, I've worked in financial sales, an area that has endured many challenges because of economic shifts. In the beginning, I scraped by, making just enough to keep my job and pay my bills. While I was merely surviving, I saw others who were thriving. Frankly, I was tired of being at the bottom of the sales chart, but I didn't know where to turn to find a way upward.

Then I introduced my sister-in-law, Hanni, to the same career and taught her everything I knew about the business.

I expected that Hanni would face the same obstacles I had been experiencing.

I was wrong – and surprised.

Hanni launched herself almost immediately into a successful sales career. In just eight months, she clinched a prestigious sales award in the company and qualified for the annual sales-convention challenge – something I had not yet achieved, but yearned for.

I watched Hanni scale the rungs of the sales ladder. She seemed to possess the Midas touch – every effort turned to gold. I thought to myself,

She has the same skill set and knowledge as I do. Why is she so successful when I am just getting by?

Spurred by her stunning performance, I learned from my own student. I discovered what she had uncovered – the lessons that sales managers never see fit to teach you. I started achieving sales conferences and awards annually. I belong to the top 10% of the sales distribution channel and then I was promoted to be one of the youngest sales managers by age of 26, heading up a team of 12 sales people.

For some people, these insights come naturally. For others, like me, they are delivered in a series of "aha!" moments that change the entire course of your career.

I wrote this book to help other sales professionals seize opportunities that were previously either unavailable or unseen. I decided to share my eleven secrets in a story format to make it more interesting and compelling. Storytelling is, after all, an important ability for a salesperson to have (see Chapter 9 on the power of persuasion).

The knowledge in *What Your Sales Managers Never Teach You* will help you take control of your own success rather than rely on standard sales training or guesswork. I applied every single lesson to my own work, and each one contributed to making me a better sales professional, a better manager, and a better leader. Currently, I am in a role in partnership and distribution, working closely with sales leaders to achieve sales targets. I love my career and the vast opportunities it presents. When you taste success, you will always hunger for more, and this book will give you a full menu of possibilities.

Good luck! And please share your thoughts and stories with me at www.mustreadsalesbooks.com.

—Kevin Foo

Chapter 1

The Eight Rules of Engagement

Before I start this story of sales-success secrets, I want to lay out some ground rules. In the interest of transparency and authenticity, there are some things you should know about my experience, my insights, and me.

1. **I might not be right.** I'm giving you my perspective based on my experience. I've been in sales for over a decade and have enjoyed success after a shaky start. I believe that what worked for me will work for you, but we are all entitled to our opinions.

2. **It's not just my knowledge.** I would never take credit for the brilliance of others! The thoughts and practices I am offering here are based on my personal experiences and include knowledge and ideas I gained from other people.

3. **Intelligence does not make you smart.** Let's be clear here. You can be highly intelligent in terms of your IQ and academic training, but "street smarts" are often gained by setting aside what you've learned in a book or classroom and opening your mind to new ideas. We may not be the most intelligent people on the planet, but we can choose to be among the smartest!

4. **We are all students.** Every day is – or should be – a learning experience. Keep searching for knowledge. You will soon discover that the more you know, the more you need to learn. There is always room to grow.

5. **I do not teach; I only share.** I do not profess to be the ultimate source of knowledge on the topic of sales. I am sharing insights here with the hope that you can apply them to your life and make the most of them.

6. **Experience is not right or wrong.** What I offer to you here comes from what I have seen or done. I am a witness and participant at the same time. I am sharing the good and the bad, the right and the wrong, and hoping that my experience will help you to avoid such missteps in your own career.

7. **Keep the best and toss the rest.** You might not agree with everything I'm suggesting, and that's fine. My goal is to serve up the ideas so that you have options and action points for expanding your sales performance. Take the ideas that fit your personality, style, and goals. Discard any that are not applicable to you. All I ask is that you at least consider the possibility and question yourself before rejecting it.

8. **Share.** If you show improvement as a result of these ideas, please share. If these lessons spawn other tips or stories, I want to hear about them too. You can reach me at (URL or email).

With this in mind, let's get going on opening up some opportunities to become the sales star you envisioned when you started your career!

Chapter 2

Waking from the Sleepwalk

"Awareness before change"

The alarm clock chimed in Michael's ear, but he was so accustomed to the shrill sound that he barely moved, reaching one hand from under the covers to hit the snooze button.

Another Monday morning.

Michael laid there with his eyes still closed, refusing to surrender to the daylight. He thought about the day and the week ahead. He tried to muster the excitement he once felt, back when he was certain he would scale the ladder of the financial-services industry. Back in those days, he had felt destined for success, certain he had the talent to soar past others on his way to the top. He had estimated it would take two years, maybe three.

Here he was three years later, and he was still mired in the same place he'd been for far too long – and still so far short of his goals. He'd done well enough to keep his job and earn a decent income, but had failed to make sufficient progress toward achieving his dream. Michael was confident that he was smart enough. After all, he'd graduated in the top 10 per cent of his class at business school. He certainly had the ambition. When he first arrived at this company, he was like a racehorse bursting out of the starting gate

What had happened? Why was he still sitting on this frustrating plateau, unable to close more deals and live up to the potential he had? Or at least he *used to think* he had the right potential. His confidence had waned in his failure to progress.

Even more frustrating was seeing his protégée, Vivian, living out *his* dream. She came on board six months ago, and he was assigned to train her in the company's processes and get her started. Well, she got started all right. Then she took off. He hated to admit it, but Vivian was already a better salesperson than he was. He just hoped that no one else had caught on to that. It would be the ultimate humiliation to fall behind his mentee.

His wife, Ellie, slept peacefully beside him. She wouldn't be up for another hour. Michael envied her that extra hour of sleep.

The alarm sounded again. This time, Michael fumbled with the clock and hit the off button. He sighed, kicked back the covers, and slowly pushed himself out of bed. It felt like a major chore to get going every morning, like the springs in his joints had become un-sprung.

I've got to get myself back to the gym, he mumbled to himself.

It had been almost a year since he'd last worked out. Had it really been that long? It used to be a regular part of his daily routine, but even that activity had lost its lustre.

He'd most certainly caved in to the "Why bother?" excuse far too often. A little voice inside his head was trying to wake him up, but he dismissed the message. It was so much easier not to deal with problems and hope they'd just go away.

Michael showered, shaved, and dressed. He stumbled through his routine with no energy, going through the motions like a robot. He grabbed his briefcase and a toaster pastry from the pantry. No time to warm it up. That would take too much time and he was already almost ten minutes behind schedule.

Let's just hope there's no traffic on the way.

But there was always traffic at this time of day and Michael knew it. Fortunately, no one ever seemed to notice that he was often a few minutes late. One nice thing about his job – so many team members were coming and going throughout the day, no one could tell if he was late. There were breakfast meetings that make people late, and dinner meetings that took them out of the office a bit earlier than usual. Although Michael had precious few of those meetings, he figured he would blend right in by not sitting at his desk from eight-thirty to five every day.

*****

The traffic was actually a bit lighter than usual, particularly for a Monday morning which was when most commuters seemed to have trouble getting to work on time. Although he should have already been at his desk, Michael stopped at the coffee shop in the lobby of his office building to get his morning jolt of caffeine – with a double espresso shot on Monday.

He rode the elevator to the twenty-third floor while making mental notes about his day. Who did he need to call? Which prospects should get a little nudge this morning? He decided to spend an hour making calls and trying to schedule appointments for the week, because he knew his calendar had some gaping holes to fill.

When he stepped off the elevator and headed toward his office, he saw Vivian already at her desk. She was on the phone, talking with incredible energy for this time on a Monday morning and was tapping away at her keyboard.

As Michael walked by, he noticed she seemed to have systems set up for everything. It all appeared to be neatly organized – a binder for each client, file folders which organized tasks by priority, a laptop, a notepad, and a tablet. He could see her calendar on her computer screen. It was colour-coded – green for prospects, blue for clients, and yellow for follow-up – and looked like a vibrant mosaic. Her days were filled with tasks and appointments.

Michael thought of his own calendar and realized that, in comparison, his looked like a Christmas tree with most of the tiny lights unlit.

Seeing Vivian's passion for her work reminded Michael of the way he used to be when he was fresh from college with a degree in finance. Like

Vivian, he was anxious to use his shiny new knowledge to help people make better financial decisions and gain the security they needed and wanted. He'd been successful enough to stay in his boss's good graces, but no matter how hard he tried, he never reached the stellar levels he was seeking.

Among his yet unreached goals was the coveted membership in the company's *Pinnacle Circle of Sales Performers*. This group was comprised of the sales elite – the top 10 per cent of the sales force. Every year, Pinnacle Circle members were awarded a free trip to the annual conference, which took place at resorts in great destinations like Hawaii, Gold Coast, Paris, and Tokyo.

Michael had come close – oh so close – several times, but after three years, he had yet to achieve this dream.

His only consolation was that none of his close colleagues had achieved that level in recent years, so missing this mark was a common denominator. They'd consoled one another with the belief that this high spot is reserved for the "chosen few" in other offices. Michael's team had a more challenging territory, the economy wasn't helping, and competition was really tough.

Thus Michael came to accept his fate, and every year the image of himself enjoying a luxurious vacation, and the pride of making it into the Pinnacle Circle, became more and more blurred.

Michael was almost past Vivian's desk, when she whirled around and waved to get his attention. He didn't really want to talk to her, but she gestured for him to wait. Hurriedly, she made a new entry on her calendar – a green one, meaning another new prospect – and finished her call.

"Great! I'll see you then," she said, smiling as she tapped her headset to end the call. Vivian's eyes were bright, and her energy was so high that Michael could almost see lightning bolts shooting from her body.

"Michael, I can't believe it!" she gushed in a tone that was both excited and hushed – as hushed as she could manage, given her obvious thrill. "I got my invitation to the Pinnacle Circle conference! Can you believe it? Oh, I am *so* excited!"

Michael was stunned. How could that be? *What Vivian knew about this business – all her presentation skills and product knowledge – was taught to her by me,* he thought. The uncomfortable sensation of jealousy crept over him. *How did she manage to achieve such a high level of success within such a short period?*

Trying to compose himself, he said, "Really? Wow, that's great, Vivian. Congratulations." He stumbled, trying to sort through his thoughts. *She must be mistaken,* he thought. "I, um, didn't know you were eligible yet. Gee, that's, uh, incredible. Can I see the email?"

Vivian turned back to her computer, quickly taped the keys, and opened the email. Michael leaned closer to read the message:

> *Congratulations, Vivian. Based on your consistent record of exemplary performance, we are pleased to welcome you to the Pinnacle Circle of Sales Performers. You are also honoured as one of the Top Rookies for the year. Please mark your calendar to join us for our annual incentive trip to Hawaii this April.*

Michael read the email over again. *Vivian is in the Pinnacle Circle this year, only eight months into her sales career.* He could hardly believe it.

Faking the biggest smile he could muster, he walked back to his own workstation, booted up his computer and checked his email. Two meeting reminders, a couple of jokes from friends, a client requesting yet another change on his account, the weekly newsletter from the corporate office, and a weekly sales report from Vivian.

When Vivian started with the company, Michael requested a daily status report from her so he could see what she was doing, identify possible problems or opportunities, and basically keep an eye on the "new kid." After two months, he told her a weekly report was fine. Not long after that, he pretty much stopped looking at them at all, since she seemed to have the hang of the sales process.

As a result, he'd never noticed that Vivian was performing at such a high level. Michael clicked open the last report which Vivian had sent on the previous Friday. He noticed an impressive list of new clients and prospects, as well as a note about registering for courses to build her selling skills.

He clicked open her report from the week before. She had closed some good prospects then too. Plus, she attended some networking events and industry-related events during the week.

Michael clicked one report after another. He observed steady progress almost from the very start. To quote the Alicia Keyes song, "This girl is on fire!"

Chapter 3

The Student Becomes the Teacher

"When the student is ready, the teacher will appear"
—Chinese proverb

Michael couldn't believe what he saw in these reports. How could he have overlooked the fact that Vivian was making such great contacts – and then closing the sales? Why did he just assume that she was following the same track he'd been on? That just-getting-by track.

Even more curious, Michael scrolled down to pulled up the Vivian's very first status report. It seemed vaguely familiar. She'd identified some lofty goals. He hated to admit it now, but he remembered snickering to himself and thinking, "Yeah, good luck with that."

The fact was, this gal had achieved everything on her list – and more. Every week, her reports showed that she diligently tracked her success, sought out new opportunities, and focused on achieving what she set out to do. Even when she didn't close a deal, she made notes about a lesson learned. Notes such as:

"Need to do more research on alternatives for this prospect."

"Loyal to his current advisor. Must cultivate that in my own clients."

Once he started reading, Michael found he couldn't stop. He read every status report that Vivian sent him, most of which he'd barely glanced at before. He noted steady growth right from the start. She took risks and seemed fearless in her efforts to generate new business. She had a lot of rejections in the beginning, but she was also pursuing a high number of prospects.

Her closing ratio was low initially, but as the weeks went by, according to Michael's quick calculation of her conversion rate, grew proportionately. It had taken him three years to achieve the pitch-to-close conversion rate she'd reached in less than eight months. He also noticed that Vivian pursued more impressive targets and was snagging them.

He'd always known that Vivian was a hard worker, but still she wasn't one to put in extremely long days.

How did she do so much in a day? he wondered.

Michael had to admit that Vivian had somehow learned to work smarter, not harder. She appeared to be crystal clear on what she wanted to do – not just on a daily basis but for her entire career.

As much as it pained him to ask advice of his one-time protégée, Michael found he was eager to know more about her winning formula. Overriding his pride, he invited Vivian to his work station for a chat. She hurried in, exuding her usual eagerness to meet him.

"I don't think I properly congratulated you on your achievement," Michael started slowly. He wasn't sure how he was going to get to the point. "Getting into the Pinnacle Circle is a big deal for anyone in this firm, but getting there in your first year is really outstanding. You've done a phenomenal job."

"Thank you, Michael. I really appreciate that. I'm so excited!" Vivian's eyes were sparkling. Before this, Michael always thought her to have a bit too much exuberance, but given her success now he wondered if he'd underestimated the power of her energy.

"You know, Vivian, I've read your status reports, and it's no surprise that you've achieved this success," Michael said, not wanting her to know that he only just now read those updates. He also didn't want to admit that her success actually *was* a surprise – at least, to him. "I also want to apologize, because I don't think I've been much help to you. I was supposed to be your mentor, but clearly, you've paved your own path to success."

Vivian had been standing, but now she pulled up a chair in front of Michael's desk and sat down. "You know, I was afraid you might feel that way," she said. "The truth is, you really helped me in a way I appreciated. You did share with me all that a rookie needs to know. That, I appreciate very much!"

She paused as though she were collecting her thoughts. "The best tool you gave me," she continued, "was the freedom to explore while having you as my safety net."

She explained to Michael that she had always been a curious learner, so she felt she needed to pursue more avenues so as not to burden him.

Probably a nice way to say, "You just couldn't teach me enough!" Michael thought.

"I'm also very self-directed," she told him. "I find inspiration in many ways." From there she went on to go down a list of her various resources: personal-development workshops, sales seminars, networking groups, and lots and lots of books. She paused then and added, "I'd be happy to share what worked for me if you're interested."

"You know," he said as he tried not to choke on his swallowed pride, "you've clearly got a winning formula, and I would appreciate finding out some of those secrets that you uncovered."

She smiled, shook Michael's hand, and suggested that they should schedule a few hours to review what she called,

"What Your Sales Managers Never Teach You."

Looking a bit embarrassed she quickly said, "Oh, I'm sorry. I hope that title doesn't offend you. That phrase doesn't refer to you. It's actually something that another salesperson shared with me at a meeting once and the name just stuck with me."

Michael had to laugh. "Don't apologize, Vivian. First of all, I'm not your sales manager, and secondly, it sounds like it's right on target."

After assessing how much confidence Vivian had despite being a rookie, Michael thought,

It seems that it's not about the number of years in the business but the number of prospects a salesperson meets that determines the experience of a salesperson.

Chapter 4

Lesson 1:
Don't Ask How; Ask Why

"If you have a strong enough **why,** *the* **how** *will come along"*

M ichael confirmed what time the conference room would be available for the two of them to meet. It just so happened he was able to snag it for Friday afternoon. Most everything around the office slowed down on Fridays anyway.

To his surprise, when he got there Vivian already had snacks and soft drinks set out on the table. Michael hadn't even thought that far ahead. He could have taken care of those details. As usual, Vivian was prepared for her presentation.

After they were settled in, Vivian picked up a binder from the table. "This, she said, "is my career bible." She slid her hand over the cover, which was embellished with a collage of words she'd cut out and pasted:

- *Success*
- *Energy*
- *Effort*
- *Risk*
- *Creativity*
- *Study*

In numerous places, she had affixed the phrase, *learn and ask.*

Opening the binder, she flipped through the pages to give Michael an idea of what was collected there. She'd cut articles from the newspaper and magazines. She'd printed out pages from online sources. Dividers organized the content into subjects such as:

- *Ideas*
- *Prospecting*
- *Presenting*
- *Goal-Setting*
- *Time Management*

Another similar binder lay on the table as well. She picked it up and handed it to Michael.

"I took the liberty of making copies of the key information to get you started. Let's go right to 'What Your Sales Managers Never Teach You.'"

Opening the binder, he saw this printed on the first page

Secret #1: Don't ask how; ask why.

Almost without thinking, Michael read it out loud. "Don't ask how; ask why." It sounded fascinating, but he wasn't quite sure how that applied to him.

"I see that questioning look," Vivian said with a smile. "Here's what this means to me. It's our motivation more than our sales technique that propels us forward in the sales arena. When you have a strong enough *why,* the *how* will follow. In other words, if you want something badly enough, you've find a way to make it happen."

When Michael offered no comment, Vivian went on to share what motivated her. Her *why.*

She explained that her own motivation was two-fold:

1. Freedom to spend time doing what I want to do (my dreams and lifestyle outside the work arena)
2. The ability to help people achieve their personal financial goals

As she talked, Michael thought back to his beginning early days with the company, and he remembered the "fire in the belly" that he had – his desire to master his career and to become hugely successful.

He remembered back to the times when he and Ellie used to sit together planning things they wanted to do in their future, and how his sales career could help them achieve those dreams. That seemed long ago.

Vivian broke into his reverie. "Think about why you want success. Whatever that is – that *why* – is your motivation. When you have a powerful purpose, it will be the key driver in building a successful career. It keeps you pushing through obstacles like rejection. Rejection can often fuel the fire when the *why* is strong enough."

Now Vivian had struck a chord and Michael was nodding.

"Listen," she continued, "there are enough how-to books available to help you build your skills. The *how* can always be made better over time. Think of all the training sessions you and I have sat in on."

"A lot," he agreed.

"But, if the *why* is not strong enough, then there's no way a salesperson can sustain prolonged success, no matter how good he or she is. *Desire* is the missing element. You can't pursue any career without the desire that launches you. Motivation is what helps you face the daily rejections and keep going."

Vivian pointed to a paragraph on the page and instructed Michael to read it aloud:

> Desire is not something others can inculcate or import. It is just like the air in a balloon. For those who have it, we can feel it. For those who don't have it, their balloon will be deflated and cannot be filled with knowledge or skills imparted to them. There are enough how-to books on the

market – *How to Be Financially Successful, How to Stay Slim and Healthy*. It's not the *how* that's important. It's the *why*.

Desire is the only reason behind your action, and the only reason behind your decision.

"It doesn't matter whether you're just starting out in sales or you've been there for years," Vivian went on. "You have to understand *why* you're here and then keep reminding yourself. It's easy for salespeople to hit a plateau and then get stuck there simply because they lose sight of their desire and motivation. All they can see is a long road ahead, and there's nothing pushing them forward. Having a clear purpose gives you the emotional juice to push through adversity and obstacles that come along the way. When you have a strong enough *why*, the *how* will come."

Again Michael nodded. "I know exactly what you're talking about, because I had that motivation. And you're right – it is easy to stall out on a plateau." As he got up to refill their soft drinks he asked, "So how does one keep from getting stale?"

At that point, Vivian showed Michael how she used sticky notes with messages to remind herself of her *why*. In addition to simple sticky notes, she showed him photos she'd printed out from the Web of places she wanted to see, things she wanted to do, and even the type of house she wanted to live in someday.

"Here's yet another important aspect of the importance of *why*. In addition to knowing our own *why*, it's crucial for us to discover our clients' *why* as well. Why do they want to invest? What's their motivation?

"It would be easy to simply say, 'Well, they all want to make more money.' But why? Do they want more freedom, to retire early, to create a legacy, or to ensure financial security? Once I understand their desires, then I gear the solution to hit those targets."

Everything Vivian was telling him made sense. Her passion and excitement was contagious. Already he felt the spark of renewed energy. In no way was she trying to lecture him, she was just sharing her excitement.

It comes so naturally to Vivian, he thought. *Do I have that same commitment?*

At one time he certainly did have it. Surely it could be rekindled. But his attention was drawn back as Vivian hardly drew a breath before continuing.

"Our job as sales professionals is all about fulfilling a need or desire – a *want*. Clients don't come to us because they are anxious to hear our strategy. They want to know that we understand their goals, their *why*. They believe that if we understand that, then we have the skills to do the *how*, which is making the right decisions."

"How do you go about doing that exactly?" Michael wanted to know

"Good question." Vivian began to describe her approach when meeting with a new prospect. "I ask a lot of questions so that I can truly understand what they want me to do for them. I don't try to fit them into the solutions I already have in my portfolio, because that would be a cookie-cutter approach."

She held up her binder that was filled with her dream pictures. "You know what I discovered? I've learned that people *love* to visualize success and prosperity. They are willing to share their dreams with you. That might include:

- early retirement,
- a house by the beach,
- travel,
- time freedom,
- trusts for their grandchildren,
- or all of the above.

"The more they talk, the more you learn about their desires as well as their fears. You learn their motivation for financial planning, so you can tailor a program to help them reach those goals. Even if you're putting this client into an existing program, don't show them how they fit into this great plan you happen to have. Show how the components meet every need on their wish list."

Michael looked back at the page in his binder that Vivian had created for him. There was a paragraph that she had highlighted:

> *Desire is powerful motivation for success. It doesn't just end with fulfilling our own, but also the desires of our clients. Know the reasons for doing what you do.*
>
> * *Why do you sell?*
> * *Why do you sell for this company?*
> * *Why are you selling this product?*
> * *Do you believe wholeheartedly or are you just trying to make a buck?*
>
> *The best sales professionals have genuine passion for selling – and it's not just in hitting a sales goal, but in successfully serving the needs of their clients. If you do that, then you'll meet and exceed your quota. If you put the quota first, you'll struggle every single day.*

Michael carefully studied the words in front of him, soaking them up as the value of these statements filled his mind. He thought about Vivian and how she emulated every thought here. She had this passion. It made him realize that lately his focus had been on his struggle to meet sales goals and not on meeting the needs of his clients. Thinking back, he wondered at what point he'd gotten things so turned around.

Vivian then explained to Michael how she created a profile of every client. She made notes of everything she knew about each one. That might include name, age, job income level, marital status, family background, current financial portfolio and financial goals are all mandatory as part of the fact finding process for clients.

It is the "softer" data, that makes the difference, such as desired lifestyle during retirement, estate distribution, the hot buttons to ensure a standard of living or education funds if the client has passed on

Now Michael was duly impressed. He could never remember a time, even in his best selling days, when he had paid that much attention to the details of his clients. Or even his potential clients.

Vivian turned to a page in her binder where she had written the following list under her *goals* tab. She turned the book around so Michael could read it.

- Connect (reconnect) with clients regularly
- Learn the desires and motivators for clients by asking questions
- Tailor the solution to their goals
- Focus on clients
- Become a trusted advisor and start asking for referrals

Vivian paused then. "I'm talking a lot aren't I. Am I unloading too much?"

"No. Not at all. But hold on just a second." Michael already had his laptop open. Now he opened a new spreadsheet and quickly set up his own client profile. "I plan to start using this right away."

Vivian was smiling. "Good for you."

So now his homework consisted of two different, but closely related areas.

He needed to go back and remind himself why he wanted to be a success in this business – and then create reminders both at home and at the office.

He would now go back to all of his existing clients and get to know them better by creating profiles for each one.

When he got home that night, Ellie asked him, "What's going on with you? I've not seen you this happy coming home from work for a very long time."

"I think you're going to be seeing it a lot more in the future," he told her as he gave her a hug. "By the way, where are those *dream plans* you and I charted out a few years ago? I think it's time we got them out again."

Chapter 5

Lesson 2: When You Lose, Don't Lose the Lesson

"The seed of adversity, when sown in the right soil, will bear the fruits of opportunity"

Michael and Vivian decided that Friday afternoons would work best for their weekly meetings. When they met in the conference room the following Friday, Vivian again had things all laid out and ready.

"The name of the second lesson," she told him as they filled their plates with snacks, "is this: *When You Lose, Don't Lose the Lesson.*"

She showed him this section in the binder that she'd created for him. On the first page she'd written these phrases:

Lessons not learned will be repeated.
Mistakes are opportunities. Build on them.

"Most people look at mistakes as failures," Vivian told him.

Michael was already nodding his agreement. He'd made a bunch of them along the way. Especially this past year.

She went on to explain "A mistake (or a misstep) is not really a *miss*. Instead, every misstep is an opportunity to get stronger, smarter, and better! Here, look at this." She turned the page in his binder and pointed to a diagram.

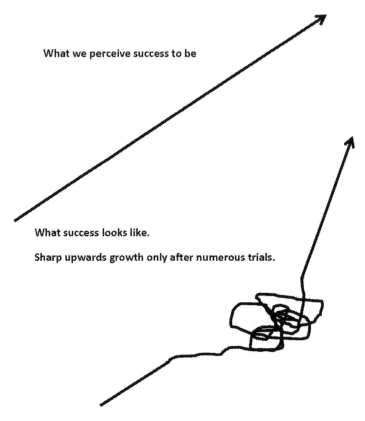

What we perceive success to be

What success looks like.

Sharp upwards growth only after numerous trials.

"Success is never walked out in a straight line," she told him, "even though we wish it were that way. There are *lots* of trials and errors along the way. Even after learning, we all need time to break into the next phase."

Vivian paused then and asked him -- almost challenged him – to think about some of his past mistakes.

It certainly didn't take much to bring several to mind. He thought about times when the client wasn't ready to invest; or when he and the client didn't connect on a personal level; or when he didn't uncover the client's motivation in making a decision. He thought about a number of such incidents, then gave himself a healthy reality check. What should he have learned from each of those encounters?

As Michael began to share a few of these experiences, they spent the next few minutes going over each one individually.

She encouraged him to answer the following questions about each one:

- What happened?
- What did I want to happen?
- What should I have done to make that happen?
- What will I *not* do again?
- What is the lesson learned from this misstep?

He thought for a minute, and then came up with these lessons learned:

- Ask more and better questions to get better insight into the client's need and wants
- Talk less, listen more
- Don't give up so easily
- Get input and advice from others rather than let pride hold me back

As had happened during their previous meeting, Michael was already thinking about how he might apply these lessons right away in his business dealings. He also realized that he should have asked his sales manager to guide him a bit more. Perhaps he should have asked the manager to come along and observe his presentations.

He knew why he didn't take that route. Again, it was his pride—he didn't want to appear unsure of himself. Then he remembered that Vivian had asked him to come with her several times, and he'd never questioned her confidence; he'd actually appreciated her desire to learn and improve.

Next, Vivian told Michael to think about one of his biggest successes and then to go through a similar process with these questions:

- What happened?
- What did I want to happen?
- What did I do to make that happen?
- How can I use that to my benefit?
- What is the lesson learned from this success?

She reminded Michael that he needed to be vigilant about paying attention to the details. "With each mistake," she said, "I take the time to analyse it. What went wrong? What could I have done to prevent it? What could I have done better to mitigate the problem? Then I make notes in my journal, writing down my thoughts and answers. Writing things down has a way of reinforcing the ideas in your mind."

As they talked, another incident came to mind which Michael shared with Vivian regarding one of his recent selling experiences. He was trying to close a deal with a potential client, but the client ended up going with a more familiar salesperson.

"Then the same thing happened with another prospect, and I thought to myself, 'Wait! What am I missing here?' I thought about other ways to handle this type of rejection. I'm confident I can convince my client that my knowledge and ability are valuable enough to overcome any objections."

"Ah," Vivian said as she began clearing off the table, "this is perfect. What you brought up is a great example of what we're going to touch on for our next lesson. So we'll table that for now. You have more than enough to keep you busy until next Friday."

She was absolutely right. Michael was already getting excited about putting into action what he'd already learned in their first two sessions.

Chapter 6

Lesson 3:
The Deal Before the Deal

"There is no deal until your prospect allows you to have a deal"

In the weeks following Michael's first two sessions with Vivian, he'd been extremely busy. However, he noticed a different *feel* about the busy-ness.

Most of it amounted to review work – going back over his lists of clients and potential clients and updating, and expanding, their profiles; then steadily sorting through past clients with whom Michael felt he had failed. Now he was ready to assess each one and determine what he could have done differently. And indeed, what he *would* do differently in the ensuing weeks.

Remembering back, he recalled an incident where a prospect had told him to call back in a few weeks. As a rookie, this invitation to reconnect gave him a sense of excitement and confidence. In his mind, the deal was as good as his. To his dismay, when he did call back the prospect had already chosen someone else to handle the investments. He didn't even get a chance to put in a proposal.

That incident affected him more deeply than he cared to admit. His response was to ignore it and pretend it never happened. It was too uncomfortable to even think about. After listening to Vivian at their last session, he wondered how things might have gone differently for him if he'd spent time and effort to dissect the incident and get to the root of what when wrong.

By the time the next Friday rolled around – time for their third meeting – Michael was pleasantly surprised to realize that for the past few days, he had not experienced that *drugged* feeling upon awaking each morning. Being more focused seemed to infuse him with energy. He couldn't really explain it, but he could sure sense it.

For this meeting, Vivian suggested they meet at the first-floor cafeteria. "We don't want to get into a rut of sameness," she told him. But Michael was convinced Vivian would never get stuck in a rut of any kind – ever.

When they arrived at the cafeteria door, Vivian told him to grab a table. She wanted to get a sandwich because she had two back-to-back meetings that evening and she might not have time to eat. Michael knew Ellie was cooking so he just grabbed a coffee and a piece of fruit.

Once they were settled at their table and Vivian had her materials out, she told him the title of this lesson: *The Deal Before the Deal.*

"That sound a little like doublespeak. I'll need an explanation on this one."

"I'm prepared to do exactly that. You may find the answer to your question from last week in today's lesson. You mentioned about an incident where a prospect left you dangling, then chose another financial advisor. Let's see what could have been set in place to prevent that from happening.

"While *deal before the deal* may sound confusing, it simply refers to the need to pre-qualify your client. It can happen like this."

Vivian pulled out a blank sheet of paper and made a few scribbles as she talked. Ask the client a defining question like this:

> *Mr. Prospect, if I'm willing to spend quality time learning about your needs and will invest professional hours to develop a personalized financial plan just for you, do you feel it would be fair for me to expect you to place your business with me?*

Michael was a little taken aback. He wasn't sure he could ask such a direct question. He'd never tried such a strategy before. He had to admit though, it did sound like wisdom.

If Vivian noticed his discomfort, she chose to ignore it. She simply took another bite of sandwich and continued.

"It's your prerogative to ask for and expect this kind of committal from a prospect. After all you are an expert in your field, and your time is valuable."

Michael nodded his agreement.

"Another such *deal-before-the-deal* technique is this. Ask the prospect exactly what time she wants you to get back with her regarding the proposal she has requested. Expect a response, and pin it down. This will give you an idea of the sense of urgency – or the lack thereof. Let the prospect see you entering that follow-up date information into your calendar. These are what I call *indicators*. They set the stage for you to proceed."

This plan sounded both scary and exciting to Michael. He could see how it could guide the prospect into making a firm commitment to take things to the next level. "Using this kind of language," he said, "would transform the request for followup from a begging stance over to a serious, confident stance."

"Exactly," Vivian said. "You're catching on quick. Asking for this kind of commitment from the prospect shows that you're not playing games or wasting time."

She went on. "This, of course, is only half of the formula. We then must put forth our full commitment to make the clients feel that they are making the right financial decision with someone they can trust and be comfortable with."

All of this was piquing Michael's interest greatly. "Now I'm wondering," he said, "do you always convert prospects into clients with this approach?"

"No system or strategy is ever going to be perfect. I think you realize that. My goal isn't to win everyone over; my goal is to work smarter and not harder. I want to try to avoid chasing after clients who are simply making excuses and have only a mild interest in what I have to offer them."

"So you're increasing the odds of the ones that are more ready to commit to serious followup. Right?"

"You've got it. Why spend hours researching to create an awesome financial-plan-package for someone whose interest is half-hearted at best. The better, wiser choice is to invest that same amount of time in someone who appears eager to hear what you have to say, and to look over what you have to offer."

Vivian finished her sandwich and pushed the empty plate out of the way. Going back to her notes, she said, "We can only start to fact-find, or start the prospecting process, once the client gives us permission."

"So that's what you mean by the *deal before the deal.*"

"Yes. And more importantly, we can learn to also influence the outcome by making the client like us first – before anything else. Remember, it's not what you know, but how you make the prospect feel that makes the difference. They have to first like you, then trust you, and finally *maybe* decide to do business with you. It's the universal law of the business world – nobody likes to do business with someone they do not like or trust."

"That sounds like one of those things that easier said than done," Michael said. "So what's the *trick* to make people like you?"

"It's not a trick, really. I have seen that many salespeople forget (or they never knew) how to connect with a prospect as a friend. Instead, in their mind, this is a *target,* or a *goal,* or another stepping stone on the way to their monthly sales target. The result is a tone of aloofness, distance, and disconnect."

Michael could almost feel himself blushing. "I've done that," he admitted. To himself he thought, *I've done it way too many times.*

Vivian ignored his discomfort. "Talk to your clients and prospects as though you were connecting with an old friend. Be honest. Be sincere. Begin to train yourself to think of their welfare rather than your sales figures."

Before they left the cafeteria that Friday afternoon, Vivian left Michael with a few more thoughts.

- Regarding the follow up, ask for their permission for the reconnect. Let them set the date and time. Never leave it as an open option – or worse – an open-ended guessing game.

- By asking for a follow-up timeline, you have now effectively measured a sense of urgency from the prospect – whether they are ready to take action from the discussion we have just concluded.

- Now take the initiative to follow up with articles or events that they may be interested in personally, by mail or e-mail. (Did you find out their favourite sport? Then comment on the most recent national game.) This lets them know that you do care about them.

- Never let "out of sight, out of mind" eradicate all the effort you put into this initial meeting. Find a reason to connect with the client *before* the next followup meeting.

- At the followup meeting, remember, *if you're not early you're late*. Arrive a little before you said you would. Punctuality can make a big impression.

As they walked out of the cafeteria, Michael said, "Thanks again, Vivian. I'm ready to go back and analyse some of my missteps from the past and make note of lessons I can learn from each one."

"Good for you," she said as she breezed through the door he held open for her. "After all, life is a succession of lessons. With each one, we're climbing a step on the ladder to success. The higher we get, perched up on the knowledge we've already gained, the farther we can see – all the way past the mistakes and on to the opportunities ahead."

Chapter 7

Lesson 4: Back to Better Basics

"Are we busy, or are we productive?"

M ichael told Vivian that he was in charge of their fourth meeting. He ordered sushi from the deli down the street, and also had a folder full of notes to show her. When she stepped into the conference room, it was his turn to be early and have everything ready.

As with other areas in his life, Michael was becoming much more assertive and proactive in everything he did. This included making weekly prospect calls to schedule presentations. He'd already made lunch appointments with two previous clients and managed to overcome objections from a tough prospect that he'd almost given up on. That presentation was scheduled for the following week, and he knew that by that time, he'd have gained even more valuable lessons from Vivian.

Because of his coaching session with Vivian, Michael is beginning to feel the zeal and excitement that he'd had in his early days with the company. Only now it was more of an *educated excitement* as opposed to a *blind novice* excitement. He had renewed hope that he could actually become the sales professional he always dreamed of becoming.

As they ate from the sushi tray, Michael took the opportunity to update Vivian on all his recent activities. The fact was, the two of them were so busy during the week, they didn't have much time to compare notes. So by Friday, Michael had a number of successes to share.

"And now," Vivian said, as she opened the binder, "we're ready for, *Back to Better Basics.*"

Tapping the words on the page, she said, "Here's something I wish I'd learned *before* I started selling. To succeed in selling – no matter *what* you're selling – you have to accept that there are no shortcuts. Work hard and work smart. Learn the trade, not the tricks of the trade."

She reached over and turned the page in Michael's notebook. She pointed to four words on the page that she had circled in red:

- Productivity
- Proficiency
- Profitability
- Purpose

"These are the four things you need to focus on. Together, they empower you," Vivian explained. "More often than not, it's not proficiency that kills a sales career. Lack of productivity is the real assassin. You can be extremely proficient at selling, but if you aren't productive with your time, you won't achieve your potential."

"Boy does that hit home," Michael said. He was thinking about all the *stall tactics* that he had perfected in the past few months. It bothered him that he seemed to stay busy, but got so little done. But he was never sure what to do about it.

"I have a friend named Kenneth," Vivian went on. "Kenneth is also in sales but in another industry. When I first met him, I was a bit awed by him, because he's an extremely effective salesperson and a great closer. He closes about one out of every two deals he has on the table."

"That's pretty good averages if you ask me."

"I thought the same thing. But then Kenneth told me that he wasn't meeting his goals."

"What? Closes one out of every two deals, but can't make his goals? That doesn't make sense."

"I agree. So I asked him how that could be possible. He told me that he *ran out of those **twos**.*"

Michael looked confused, so she explained. "Kenneth was proficient at closing, yes. He closed one of out every two deals, yes. But know what the problem was? He didn't have enough opportunities; he didn't have enough deal to close. He was good for one out of two, but when there weren't enough **twos**, he had nothing to apply his proficiency to."

"Aha." Now Michael saw her point. "No matter how good you are at closing, if you don't have enough deals to close it's doing you no good. So in essence, Kenneth was proficient, but not too productive."

"Right. Being *productive* with your time, and making a major effort to generate prospects, is one of the major factors in succeeding at sales. If you want more sales, you have to be more productive in finding prospects. Focus on getting the number of cases in, focus on the basics, before going for the larger cases, the profitability part of the formula."

Vivian opened her laptop and clicked to a screen with her calendar. "Look here," she says, pointing to the *Lunch* column on next Monday's schedule. It says *Lunch with colleagues.*

How Most Sales Person Schedule Look Like

	monday	tuesday	wednesday	thursday	friday	saturday	sunday
Morning	Coffee or Breakfast With Colleagues					REST	REST
Afternoon	Lunch With Colleagues						
Evening	Fixing Appointments & Appointments With Prospects Only						

How Your Weekly Schedule Should Look Like

	monday	tuesday	Wednesday	Thursday	Friday	saturday	sunday
Early Morning	New Business Submission or Prepare Call List						REST
Early Afternoon	Fixing Appointments for the week		Appointments With Clients/ Prospect				
Afternoon	Lunch With Clients/ Prospects						
Late Afternoon	Fixing Appointments for the week		Appointments With Clients/ Prospect				
Evening	Fixing Appointments for the week & Appointments With Clients/ Prospect						

"See that?"

Michael nodded.

Vivian highlighted the three words and hit the delete button.

"Know why I delete that entry?"

"I think I have a good idea."

"I don't sell to my colleagues."

Michael smiled. He was pretty sure that was what she was going to say.

"I made up my mind at the outset that I would not spend important sales time on my colleagues. Instead, I *invest* that hour or two in something that gives me a solid return. I'll have lunch with someone who has the possibility of becoming a client, becoming a bigger client, or referring a client to me."

Michael thought about his usual lunch plans. He nearly always lunched with his co-workers. In fact, he had two on his calendar for the upcoming week. Now he was wondering, *Is it bad form to back out*?

"Once the productivity and proficiency are in place, the third part of the success equation is *profitability*. Profitability factors into productivity," Vivian explained. "As I referred to earlier, it's not enough to be busy, you must learn to be efficient with your time, making sure you invest it wisely."

"Like avoiding lunch with colleagues who are not clients and gives no return," Michael added with a smile.

"Exactly."

"Well, I can tell you right now that I fall way short when it comes to budgeting my time wisely."

"I like that you used the word *budget*. I like to think of budgeting my time just like I budget my finances – with both short- and long-term results in mind."

Closing her laptop and moving it aside, Vivian brought the binder to place it in front of them. "So now let's talk about Back to Better Basics. Keep in mind there a difference between learning the tricks of the sales trade and learning the trade itself. The *basics* that I'm talking about refer to daily tools that stimulate productivity so we can gain more of those twos."

She pointed to a chart on the page in the notebook. Here was a list of simple adjustments that can be made to daily habits. It was things like:

- Administration, such as new business submission, etc.
- Prepare calling list
- fixing up weekly appointments
- Planning to have lunch with prospects – or existing clients who can offer referrals.

"Every week my goal is to have my week booked – every week. I want my calendar full of appointment, with no open times. Open times to me represent wasted opportunities."

Michael couldn't help but think of how empty his own calendar had been of late. It was embarrassing and made him feel guilty. Now he was seeing why. He'd not mastered his own calendar.

"Control the controllable," Vivian continued. "Activities are within your control. Be the master of your time, not the other way around. When you don't manage your calendar, time slips away, and with it goes opportunity. Can you afford to give those opportunities to another salesperson who is more in control? I assure you, I am *always* happy to get more leads that others have overlooked."

Michael thought of several colleagues who regularly enjoyed long lunches together. There had been times when he secretly wished he was on the inside track with those co-workers. But Vivian's admonition makes him realize he was much better off using that time to further his career.

"Here's another perspective that may help you. Think of Wednesday as the *most* important day of the week." The laptop came back open and Vivian pointed to a graphic on her calendar screen:

Mon **T**ues **W**ed **T**hurs **F**ri **S**at **S**un

"One of my "secrets is that my week is a full seven days, unlike others whose may be a five- or six- day week." She covered over Monday and Tuesday with her fingers. "If we don't work on scheduling early in the week, we get to Friday and haven't accomplished our goals. If your weekly schedule is not filled up by Wednesday, even your calendar will tell you WTF!"

Michael responded with a loud chuckle. It might be off-color, but it was something he wouldn't forget. He knew for sure he hadn't been organized with his time. His calling and appointment setting was haphazard at best, making a few calls a day. When Friday rolled around, suddenly he felt the panic and the pressure. So he scrambled for more appointments. But there was always difficulty getting in touch with people on Friday. Those he did reach nearly always asked him to call back early the following week. Vivian's approach was a much more effective approach. She went on to show him how most salespersons create their own roller coaster:

Always have a scheduled calling day. If not, the appointments and closure will be a roller coaster.

Here's a typical call schedule:
- 1st week – focus on calling… many appointments on the 1st and 2nd week.
- 2nd week – focus on going for appointments, and administration of closed cases
- 3rd week – empty week – start calling cycle again.
- 4th Week – Appointments

Cycle continues.

That's the reason, why some months are better, some months are not. Calling cycle affects the productivity of the month.

Number of appointments will drop the following week.

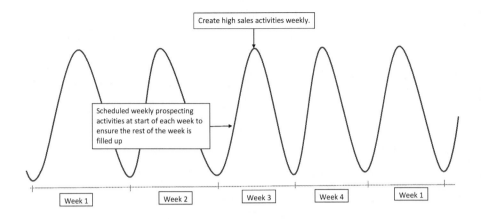

Michael opened the calendar on his Smartphone, scheduled a block of time the following Monday for working on prospecting, and then marked it as a repeating event for every Monday.

"Typically," Vivian continues, "clients ask for the same time and day for a rescheduling or a follow-up. That makes it all the more important that we fix it earlier in the week, so our monthly schedule can be managed as such." Vivian tapped her fingers onto a diagram she had drawn on her notebook.

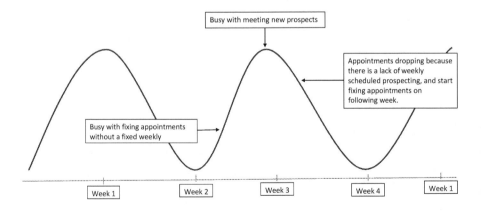

"Delaying your appointment-fixing to the latter part of the week will have a tremendous negative impact on your month productivity. It reduces your productivity by one week in total."

Michael nodded. This plan made so much more sense. He could see the long-range benefits and felt his old excitement beginning to rise.

"Now that you know how to fix up your schedule, how's your calling coming along this week?" Vivian asked.

"Er uh, … good, I suppose. However, many of my prospects were not available when I tried contacting them," Michael replied.

"I'm not trying to point fingers here, but do I sense some call reluctance?"

Michael knew she'd hit a sore spot with him. He nodded. "A little reluctance I guess you could say."

Vivian was quick to say, "Hey, no need to feel bad about that. I'd say most every salesperson feels the same way. It's just that some feel it more than others. May I suggest a simple and effective calling exercise to you?"

Michael nodded, interested to hear what she'd come up with next.

"Think about when you visit the gym," she said. "What does the fitness instructor say? 'Just complete the same amount of sets.' However, as we start building strength and improving, the quantity of the sets increase. That's the little secret that I stole from my fitness instructor," Vivian said with a laugh.

"Initially, my instructor started me with ten reps of four sets; now, I have progressed to fifteen reps of four sets. Calling can be grouped into sets too. This is how I start."

Vivian grabbed a plain piece of paper from her briefcase. She then folded it into four equal quadrants. "I start with geographical sets of ten prospects within each quadrant. This helps me to save travel time and be more effective in managing my time. And I get to meet multiple prospects within an area.

"After each quadrant – or you can call it a set – I take a quick five-minute break. Get myself refreshed and start with my next set until I complete it all. Effectively, I have prospected forty new leads."

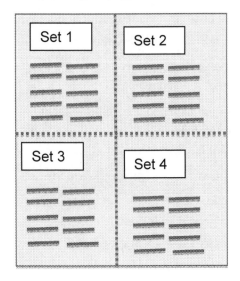

She handed Michael the paper and continued, "At this point, I break down the ten prospects within each set and segment them into prospect net worth. I choose a mix to help me balance my appointment times. I know that the prospect with a higher net worth may need more time to convert due to larger ticket size; the lower net-worth prospect looking at smaller ticket items, will require a shorter sales cycle."

Michael was amazed. He'd never looked at his call list like this before. "Wow. I didn't know that by simply breaking my list into sets, I could potentially achieve so much more!"

"You can create so many variations of this concept," Vivian told him. "From geographical, to net worth, to a specific occupation class. And yet another added benefit – this method of calling helps you to see which market-segment is giving you the greatest and best results. With that information you can then be more focused on the segment that buys the most from you!"

"And that kind of focus can increase sales volume." Turning the folded piece of paper in his hands, Michael was already imagining how he was going to start right away to segment his calling by using this method.

"And higher sales volume also means helping more people," Vivian said with a smile. "That's the part I like best." She closed her laptop and tucked it back into the case. "So," she asked, "what do you think about this method of calling?"

"I'm fascinated. I would say it's really back to *better* basics."

"It's time to challenge yourself to a no-blank week."

"No-blank week?"

"Yes! Set a goal of submitting a sale every week. Focus on the activity, not the size of the sale – because as professional salespeople, that's what we can control. Agree?"

Michael nodded.

"If you want, we could challenge each other for the next eight weeks for a no-blank week. You game for that?"

"I'm game! Let's go for it." Michael offered a handshake to take on her challenge. "Let's start this week!"

"The law of quality will govern us," Vivian said in summing up their talk. "Build a system, a habit. Systematize your basic activity and humanize the process. Start with a simple process for you to kick-start. From there you can build up after you follow up. And remember, simple does not mean easy. Let's tally our score at the end of eight weeks."

"It's a deal."

Chapter 8

Lesson 5: The Million-Dollar Deal

*"There is no difference between selling to a wealthy person
and a man on the street. The difference is
only the salesperson himself"*

"Hey, Michael, come on. We're all going out for lunch!"
Michael's colleague, Andrew, broke into Michael's
concentration. He was just starting to read the next lesson in his binder in
preparation for the next's week coaching session with Vivian. It looked like
powerful subject: "Dream: How to Get That Million-Dollar Deal."

Michael looked at the clock on his computer and heard the grumbling
of his hungry stomach calling for food. He closed the binder and shut his
laptop. As he pushed back from his desk and stood to leave, Vivian's advice
from their previous session resonated in his head:

> *Don't waste lunchtime dining with colleagues and friends.
> They're not going to buy from you.*

He looked past Andrew and saw that Vivian was preparing to leave. She
grabbed her tablet and her client's financial portfolio, so he assumed she
wasn't going to grab lunch, at least not with any colleagues. Vivian was most
likely making good use of her time by seeing a prospect or client.

"Are you coming or what?" Andrew asked impatiently.

"You know what?" Michael said, returning to his seat. "I've got things I should do, so I'll pass for this time."

"Okay," Andrew shrugged. "Your loss."

As Andrew disappeared into the hall, Michael opened the binder again and whispered to himself, "No, *my gain*."

*****

At their next meeting Michael told her how he was turning down lunch invitations and how empowered it made him feel – and how much he was able to accomplish during that time.

As they were arranging their materials out on the conference table, Michael admitted he'd read ahead in the materials. "I'm interested because I've noted that you've been extremely successful in closing the bigger deals."

He pulled out a sheet of paper and laid it on the table between them. It was a copy of Vivian's last status report. He pointed to the names under the column labelled, "Prospects."

"You have some heavy hitters here, Vivian. This guy," he said, pointing to the name of a well-known entrepreneur.

"He's a great guy," Vivian says. "And a wonderful referral source. He's already sent me two other people who have become valuable clients."

"How do you get your foot in the door with these high-level types?" Michael asked her.

"That's exactly what we're going to talk about this afternoon," Vivian told him. "Do you know the difference between selling to a higher net worth person and a man on the street?"

Michael shook his head.

"Think about it."

"Well," he said, trying to be a good student and give her the right answer, "their goals are certainly more complex, so the strategy has to be, too. And I'm sure it's a lot harder to get to them."

Vivian looks at Michael, nodding slightly. "That's true, to a degree. But there's one big difference."

"The price of the lunch?" he replied, trying to crack a joke. The truth was he had no idea the answer.

Vivian did laugh. "Funny, she said, but not quite what I have in mind."

"Okay, I give. What *is* the difference between selling to a wealthy man and a man on the street?"

Vivian tapped the table in front of Michael and said, "You."

"Excuse me?"

"The only difference between selling to a higher net worth person and a man on the street is you – the salesperson," she said. "Think about it. When you started out, your sales manager probably encouraged you to start small. Am I right?"

Michael thought about Edward, his first boss at the firm. He was aggressive at selling and had worked his way up in the organization by steadily increasing his client portfolio. In the beginning, Edward advised Michael to start small and slowly build momentum as he gained experience. "Don't get ahead of yourself," he had warned Michael.

"When you start small," Vivian explained, "it's easy to get stuck there. You continue to think small. The longer you allow yourself to stay in this small place, the harder it is to open your mind and dream bigger. To be confident of yourself."

Vivian pointed to the status report on the table. "The reality is that the higher net worth prospects you reach for, the less competition you encounter. Don't make assumptions about big prospects being difficult people to deal with. I've found that they are impressed by go-getters, because that's exactly what *they* are."

Vivian flipped a page in her notebook and moved the binder over in front of Michael. He looks down at the page, which features a graphic entitled, "How to Go Get That $1,000,000 Revenue!"

Achieving $1,000,000 Revenue within the shortest time!

Working smart OR simply working hard?

It should be BOTH!

$1,000 revenue per case	1,000 cases
$10,000 revenue per case	100 cases
$100,000 revenue per case	10 cases

"Look at this," Vivian said, pointing to the chart. "A thousand clients or ten clients – which number is harder to get and to manage?"

"Definitely a thousand," Michael replied.

"Now let's say you had a hundred clients at $10,000 each. The total value would equal a million, right?" Vivian scribbled out the math on the back of her status report.

Michael nodded his agreement.

"But ten clients who each have a $100,000 portfolio would equal a million as well. Now, do you think that managing those ten clients would take one hundred times more effort than the thousand clients?"

Michael stared at the numbers and shook his head.

"So if you think bigger, you can make as much – no, probably *more* – money and work less. Of course, you probably wouldn't be satisfied working less, so you'd just have to make more sales. And if you did that, would you go for the smaller opportunities?"

"I never thought of it that way, Vivian. I guess I always assumed that that level of client was beyond my reach."

"My mother always told me it never hurts to ask. 'If you don't ask, you'll never know,' she used to say."

Vivian got up to get the coffee pot to fill their cups. As she did, she said, "Make a list of your current clients and a rough estimate of the net worth for each. After that, you can assign each name an *effort* factor. Assign a "1" for those who pretty much function without much work. Assign a "5" for those who require much more attention on a regular basis."

After filling their cups Vivian sat back down to wait for him to finish his list. "Okay," he said after a few minutes. "I think that's it."

"And what does that list tell you?" Vivian asked him.

Michael looked at the list. He immediately saw that he'd backed out on opportunities to network with higher-level people within his contacts. For some he didn't even dare to attempt a business conversation with them.

He pushed the list away from him and heaved a sigh. "Okay, I admit it. I've been putting too much effort into thinking small."

"You're as big as your dreams, Michael. You have nothing to lose by raising your expectations of yourself. It's fine to start small, but don't sentence yourself to staying there. Aim for being the trusted advisor of those people who can reward you with the success you've come here looking to find. Learn to start mixing higher-net-worth clients into your prospects list. Don't just jump right into high-net-worth immediately. Start prospecting from the top of the pecking order. Learn their language. Learn about their aspirations. And stop short-changing yourself!"

Vivian closed her book and began clearing off the table. She paused then and said, "Oh, and just so you know, there's no difference in the price of the lunch for a bigger prospect. I've found that people who have made a lot of money aren't always so quick to spend it, nor are they impressed by others who are."

After clearing the table, she gathered her things and headed for the door. "You coming?"

"In a minute. I think is just want to sit here for a few minutes."

"Catch you later, then."

As Michael sat there in the quiet, he could literally feel his dreams growing bigger. What a lot he'd have to share with Ellie tonight.

Chapter 9

Lesson 6: Mirror

"Mirror your way to success before you innovate"

The following Friday, Vivian suggested they meet in a bookstore coffee shop located a few blocks from their office building.

When Michael arrived, Vivian was already there and had a pile of books stacked on their table.

"Is this my homework or yours?" he joked as he pulled up a chair and sat down.

"Oh, I've already read these," Vivian told him. She picked up one of the books and flipped through it. She replaced it on the pile and pushed the books toward Michael. "These are great books that belong in your library."

He thumbed through the book as Vivian pulled her binder from her bag and opened it.

"I thought this bookstore would be a good place for us to talk about the next lesson. Tonight, we're going to learn about the value of mirroring."

Michael looked up from the book and eyed Vivian curiously. "Well, I know that imitation is the sincerest form of flattery, but shouldn't we be finding selling techniques that aren't already being used? I mean, if everybody is doing the same thing, what makes one salesperson stand out?"

"Ah," Vivian said. "You're getting ahead of yourself! This is a really important lesson. When I started out in our company, I watched a lot of people. A *lot!* Including you, Michael. I took notes about behaviours and techniques that seemed to be working.

"I learned there are some great role models out there, and I emulated the successful skills they used. Modelling your skills and behavior after someone you aspire to be like is the best way to accelerate success. In other words, mirror what others do. You can be an original once you've acquired the skills and success, but you need to start somewhere."

Michael wasn't quite convinced on this point. Vivian picked up on it immediately. "Listen," she said, "we learn to do almost everything new – from kicking a football, to tying a necktie, to making a sales call – by observing and then imitating. This isn't a new concept. All I'm saying is that you should pattern your approach on methods that work, rather than going at it in a trial-and-error fashion. That's just going to waste time and potentially cost you opportunities. Remember that *productivity* means working smarter."

Vivian stood then and motioned for Michael to follow her. She walked over to the *business books* section of the store. She stopped at the shelf marked, "Sales/Selling."

"Look at this," she said, waving her hand over the shelves lined with books. "People write books about their experiences and expertise because they want to share the wisdom. It's not crazy to copy their methods. It's crazy *not* to. If someone wanted to teach you self-defence skills, you'd pay attention and copy those moves, right?"

"I definitely would."

"Well, think about mirroring as self-defence for your career, so why wouldn't you do it in sales."

He stood there for a moment scanning the titles – dozens and dozens of books on selling. *So much to learn*, he thought to himself. *Will I ever get it all? Will I ever get it right?*

Back at their table, Vivian said, "Every day brings another opportunity to learn. The people who recognize it will always blossom. Those who don't will just wither away in the darkness. Which one do you want to be?"

"I've been lax in this area. In fact, I never before realized how reading about the success techniques of others could help."

Vivian smiled. "Pick out a couple of these and buy them today. So you can get started right away."

Chapter 10

Lesson 7:
Harness the Power of Persuasion

*"When in front of your prospect, never ask a question
unless you already know the answer"*

O n the Friday afternoon of their next evening, Michael walked into
the conference room ten minutes early. He hoped to get settled in
and organized before Vivian arrived.

Success! Vivian wasn't there. He put his things on the table and went
over to start the coffee feeling a bit proud that he'd finally taken the lead
in being on time.

That little bit of pride fell short when he saw she'd already been there.
On the whiteboard mounted on the wall opposite the long conference table,
she had written:

Michael, call me.

He looked around, wondering if he'd missed something. Was this a
joke? There was nothing on the table. Did he get the time wrong? But this
was the time they always met on Fridays.

He pulled out his cell phone, found her name in his directory, and
autodialed. She answered on the fourth ring, just as Michael thought he
was about to get her voicemail.

"Hi, Michael," Vivian answered in her usual cheerful manner.

"Hey," he replied. "So, did I get the meeting time wrong? I'm in the conference room all by myself. What's up?"

"I'm not sure if I can make it this afternoon, Michael."

This seemed quite strange. "Oh. Okay. Um, shall we just reschedule?" he asked.

"Gee, I don't know. The next few weeks are looking pretty crazy for me," Vivian sounded distracted, like she was in the middle of doing something else.

This was such a surprise. She'd been so enthusiastic about coaching him. Now suddenly she seemed hesitant about moving forward.

"Okay. Well, I totally understand, Vivian. Why don't you just let me know when we can resume."

"Will do. Thanks, Michael, I've got to go now."

Vivian clicked off and Michael just stood there staring down at his phone, confused. What was that all about? Had he done something to offend her?

Michael picked up his briefcase and turned toward the door, recalling their previous session. Had he missed a sign that she was upset with him?

He looked up just in time to see Vivian standing in the conference-room doorway, blocking his exit. She smiled at his startled expression.

"Well, let me just say that this is going to be a very important session for you, Michael."

Michael shook his head, still trying to untangle his confusion. "I don't get it. What's going on?"

"Listen, Michael, here's what just happened. I was trying to see whether or not you would try to overcome my objection and convince me how important it is for us to keep working together. Tonight's session is all about the power of persuasion, so I thought I might throw in a little real-world relevance to get us started."

Vivian brushed past the still-stunned Michael and walked to the conference table. Sitting down she opened her briefcase and removed the binder. She flipped through the pages and left it open on the table. Then she walked over to the whiteboard, erased her previous message, and wrote the words *convince to persuade.*

Michael was still standing at the doorway.

"Well, are you going to come in and get started or just be irritated with me?"

Wordlessly, he walked over and sat at the conference table across from where she was standing.

"So, let's talk about persuasion, Michael. It's about influencing a person to accept your proposition, right? It's not about arm-twisting or outmanoeuvring your opponents. That's bullying and coercion, and it just doesn't lead to lasting success."

She turned back to the whiteboard and drew a big red line through the word *convince*. Above it she wrote *persuade.*

Convince ≠ Persuade

"True persuasion is about finding a solution to a conflict, creating a middle ground, and coming to a consensus of mutual benefits. Think about a news reporter who wants to get your attention. A great journalist knows that if he wants his story to be read, he doesn't just write about an accident – he writes about a *tragic* accident."

Vivian circled the word *persuade* on the board several times for emphasis. "We all need to understand and learn the power of persuasion, because it's essential in any business – particularly sales." She paused, smiling at Michael, who was now nodding in agreement.

"Okay," Vivian continued, "so what every top salesperson knows is that you never ask a question unless you already know the answer. Lead the discussion in the direction you want it to go, armed with your knowledge." She paused then waiting for him to make a response.

"Sounds easy enough. How can we make that happen?"

"Great question, Michael. Essentially there are three key strategies."

She turned back to the whiteboard and wrote:

#1 Ask the right questions

"You know what you want to learn from your prospect. You want to uncover the opportunities there. Ultimately, you want to guide that individual directly to your solution."

Michael made a note in his notebook: *Ask better questions!* Then he highlighted the phrase in yellow.

"Whenever I make a call or a presentation," Vivian continued, "I always ask myself, 'What do I want to happen? Where do I want this conversation to go?' Then I guide the other person in that direction.

"All the while, I'm considering what are the problems of this particular client that I can help solve, or take way the *pain points* in his decision-making process. I discover the outcome that he or she would like to achieve. We need to get clarity through a series of fact-findings by asking the right questions."

"And some good examples would be...?" Michael asked.

"I might ask something like: 'What are the 3 most important financial objectives that you will like to achieve?'"

"What are the areas that you will like to improve on for your current investment portfolio."

"Has your current portfolio been meeting your objectives so far?"

Michael nodded. That made a lot of sense.

Vivian suggested to Michael that he plan his questions in advance of any conversation so that he could get to the core need of that client. He wrote that in his notebook as well.

Turning back to the whiteboard she wrote:

#2 Learn to tell a story

This, she said is what we salespeople usually sound like:

The rate of return on your investment plan is a compound rate of 3.57 per cent per annum, annualized. Considering the risk-free rate in the market, the beta of this portfolio will be further adjusted to 1.125 per cent.

"Now," she said, "wasn't *that* a riveting story? Do you think you now have your prospect's full attention?"

"He's probably asleep," Michael said, smiling. He knew his presentations often sounded just like that.

Vivian went on to explain that storytelling is the basis of a strong presentation. While facts may be important, it's the story that sells.

"Nobody likes to listen to a complex concept presented with dry facts," she said. "That's why speakers often warm up their audience with a joke. So instead of that statement I just made, which would have sent the listener off into a daydream, try this:

Allow me to share with you how one of my clients, Glenn, took advantage of this situation.

"When you start off like this you have the prospect picturing a scenario, rather than trying to process numbers. You're seeing a solution in the works."

"I get it," Michael answers. "I should share a story about the solution rather than handing over the solution. Giving a clear example."

"Exactly!" Turning again to the whiteboard, she added one more sentence:

#3 Make your weakness your strength

"I think self-awareness is another important trait of a salesperson – and anyone else, for that matter. We all need to take a good look at ourselves and better understand who and what we are. In that way, we're not only tuned in to our strengths, but we become acutely aware of our weaknesses," she explained.

"For example, when Arnold Schwarzenegger first arrived in the United States from Austria, he started a bricklaying business with his friends.

Unfortunately, because of his heavy Austrian accent, not many people understood him, so he didn't get many jobs." As she talked she tried to imitate Arnold's famous accent, "Unt ya, I van to lay da bricks heah."

Michael chuckles and replies with a dismissive wave, "Hasta la vista, baby!"

"Well, Arnold realized that his accent was a weakness and tried to figure out how to get around it. Know what he did?"

"Tell me."

"Ah-nold," she says, still emulating the accent, "advertised his business as *Austrian Bricklaying Services*. He increased his prices to reflect that he was a European artisan rather than some foreigner who was hard to understand. Now, I have no idea what Austrian bricklaying is all about, but it sounds great, doesn't it? People thought so, and his business soared."

Vivian suggested to Michael that he assess his weaknesses and consider how to reshape them into strengths. "We all have weaknesses," she said. "When our goal is to persuade, we must turn those weaknesses into strengths that others can rely on.

"For example, when I just started, I had positioned myself as someone who had the latest training and information, and of course, someone who can stay focused on taking care of the limited number of clients. As we become more experienced, we may want to position ourselves as being more systematic and transfer our financial experience and expertise across a wider spectrum of the client base. And there are so many ways to position and market ourselves in different phases of our career."

Vivian went on to explain that these three strategies depend on the salesperson maintaining control of the presentation. "I've seen some salespeople who are so trained to anticipate and handle a client's objection that they answer the objection every time a question is asked. This breaks their presentation flow and hinders them from following a formatted presentation that they're familiar with."

Michael agreed. "That's happened to me more times that I can count. I feel if they're asking the question I'm obligated to answer it."

"Not necessarily. I have a technique that works for me so that I can keep to my own style of presentation flow. I simply say something like:

> *That's a great question, Mr. Client. Many of my clients have similar concerns, and I'll be coming to that shortly.*

"Then I go right back to my own presentation."

Michael was fascinated. This has never occurred to him. "So you're saying that I need not answer every question or objection as it arises."

He'd always been so intent on answering all questions and concerns, he let the conversation turn into a regular Q&A session, which totally compromised the effectiveness of his presentations.

"Answering every question as it arises," Vivian told him, "is just another indication that a lack of confidence is allowing you to lose control of the conversation. It's another part of the power of persuasion."

"Like taking control of the situation earlier this afternoon?" Michael was still mulling over how easily he'd given up when he thought Vivian wasn't meeting with him.

"Like that."

Michael looked at his notes and reviewed the points aloud:

#1 Ask the right questions
#2 Learn to tell a story
#3 Make your weakness your strength

"You've got it. Keep these in mind as you plan your next presentation, Michael. And see if you don't sense your power of persuasion growing and strengthening."

As they cleared off the table and headed for the door, Michael said, "Thanks again for everything Vivian." Then he added, "And I'm so glad you weren't really bailing out on me."

Chapter 11

Lesson 8: First sell problems, then sell solutions.

"Compress complex financial products into simple solutions. When people are confused, they will not commit"

In the weeks since their counselling sessions first started, Michael found many opportunities to put into practice many of the principles and concepts they'd discussed.

For instance, each week he was getting closer and closer to filling up his appointment calendar on Monday and Tuesday. There was no way to explain how that filled him with a fresh excitement about his work. He had also become more intentional about creating a friendship with each prospect and client he met with.

At one of his lunchtime appointment with a client (yes, he had many more lunch appointments these days) he found Vivian's advice resonating in his head as he applied the persuasion techniques to his presentation.

The prospect was a lady who owned a growing chain of upscale retail shops. He ascertained early on that her main concern regarded her retirement years. She had some high expectations of what she wanted that time in her life to look like. Immediately, Michael outlined to her the amount of saving and premiums paid that could bring her dreams to reality. He went on to further point out how an annuity plan could create a monthly cash flow during retirement.

Michael felt he had made a superb presentation; however, he failed to snag the sale. He was somewhat disappointed, obviously, and was ready to talk to Vivian about it at their next meeting.

They returned to the bookshop for their next meeting. Michael arrived early so he could use the time for extra reading. He was reading an article about the changing face of today's entrepreneurs when Vivian arrived. She dropped her briefcase next to the table then hurried to the café to order an iced coffee and a sandwich.

After sitting down across from him, Vivian took a long sip of her iced coffee, and started sharing with the usual energy that Michael had come to expect of her.

"You know, Michael, we need to leave educating to teachers. As salespeople, it's our job to highlight a client's problem."

"What do you mean?" Michael asked, closing the magazine and moving it aside.

"We're being taught to impart our knowledge to our prospects to help them make their decision," she said. "But raw courage is what is really needed in sales. The nerve to ask questions to find out more about your client. One of the most difficult skills is not technical skills but people skills.

"Spend time understanding your clients' motivation, wants, and needs, as well as their motivation to take action. At the same time, it's important to keep the presentation simple enough for the client to understand."

"Now that I've been putting some of these concepts into action, I can see what you're saying. Presentation skills are only part of the picture, right?"

"Right. We're taught in sales training, and by our sales managers, to hone and sharpen our presentation skills. Of course that's important, but see it as secondary. What's more important is our ability to understand the problems our clients are facing. Present their problem to them, and make them realize and accept..."

"...how our solution can help them solve it?" interrupts Michael with a smug look on his face.

"You're close. Very close. And you're learning fast. However, that's only part of the answer. What happens during a sales presentation for a rookie is that they keep focusing on the solution. And of course, the prospect will start focusing on the cost of implementation. Eventually, a better salesperson will come along with a more persuasive presentation, and the balance of the see-saw will be tilted slightly. However, we may still end up in a stalemate."

With that, Vivian scribbled a simple drawing out for Michael to see.

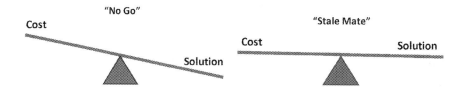

Using this see-saw as an illustration, Vivian continued to draw the next diagram.

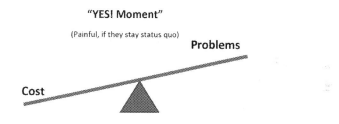

"Show them the cost of not doing anything – staying at status quo. The cost of this problem should be higher than the price of our proposed solution."

Vivian tapped on the diagram and said, "Always remember – not making a decision is also a decision. With which situation will the prospect be better off? Allow your prospect to see that indecisiveness will be costlier than making a decision to take up your solution. Whoever does that will be walking off with a signed contract." Passing the drawing to Michael, Vivian added, "Offering a solution, of course is needed; however, helping them to bring the problem into clear focus will be even more important."

Michael heaved a big sigh. "So that's it," he said.

"What's it?"

"This is why I lost a sale the other day." He went on to share with Vivian exactly what had happened with his lunch-time prospect. "I offered solutions before I brought the problem into focus – just like you said."

"In retrospect, what might you have done differently?"

Michael thought for a minute. "I guess I could have asked about her own aspirations. I could have asked her to describe her desired life style during retirement. I think she wanted to tell me, but I was too busy thinking about presenting the solutions,"

"Ah. Good insight here, Michael." She opened a new file on her computer and started typing. "Let's brainstorm for a few minutes. What questions might have worked with this client? Let's think of a few disturbing questions that are designed to stir up the client's thought process."

Between the two of them, this was the list of questions they came up with:

What will your portfolio be like by retirement time, assuming you continue what you have done?

How will you able to continue enjoy your retirement, once your money runs out in the 1ˢᵗ 10 years after you had stopped working? In other words, what's your backup plan?

What happens if you need to draw down your retirement portfolio due to unforeseen circumstances, such as accidents or illness?

How would you like it if the estate that you built up over the last 30 years is ripped apart once you passed on?

How much time will you need to pay up all the outstanding liabilities? What if time runs out for you? How will your family cope?

After their list was completed, Vivian said, "Once they've accepted their problems, only then do we offer them our solutions, which they can simply implement. Remember, Michael, learn to *sell softly.* Everyone prefers options over ultimatums. You can do this by leading the process, not pushing it."

"I had the cart before the horse, so to speak," Michael said. "I'm looking forward to implementing this lesson. I won't lose another client because of offering solutions before identifying problems. Thanks again, Vivian."

Vivian had finished off her coffee and sandwich, and was beginning to gather her things.

"Short lesson today, eh Vivian?"

"Short but powerful. Agreed?"

"Agreed."

Chapter 12

Lesson 9: Be Yourself

"Love people and use things, rather than love things and use people"

The progress Michael was making amazed even him. Each say he was getting better results. He was now making appointments with wealthier clients. Plus he had successfully made contact with six clients whom he had allowed to slip away over the past two years. And he has been finding more "twos."

He tidied up his desk, took one more glance at his calendar, and walked out to Vivian's cubicle. On her desk was a gorgeous bouquet of flowers with a note attached. Somehow, he'd never stopped to think about her having a personal life. She seemed to be too busy for such things.

Vivian was talking on the phone with her back to him. She typed something into her calendar and ended her call then turned to see Michael standing there.

"Nice flowers," he said, nodding his head toward the vase of colourful blooms, artfully arranged and tied with a bright pink bow.

"Aren't they beautiful? One of my clients sent them."

"Is it your birthday?" He wondered if he somehow missed a subtle hint that her birthday was coming up.

"Oh no, not for a while. These are from a couple who wanted to thank me for the help I gave them with figuring out how to afford early retirement.

I'm so happy for them. I could tell how anxious they were about it the last time we had dinner together."

Vivian gathered up her tablet, phone, and binder and headed for the conference room. As they entered, Michael saw that Vivian had already come up earlier and put on the coffee, and had brought in sandwiches.

Once they were settled in, she said "Tonight, I want to cover a very important topic."

"But all of the topics have been important," Michael countered. "I've gained something every single time we've met."

"That's true. But this topic is one upon which all the others will hinge."

"And that is?"

"You."

"Me?"

"Yes, you."

"Did I do something wrong? Is it this tie? I thought it might be a mistake. Ellie hates when I wear loud ties."

Vivian laughed. "No, no, no. I'm not talking about what you wear. I'm talking about you as an individual – you as a person – and how that relates to your career."

Michael feigned a nervous tug at his aforementioned tie. "Uh, this sounds a little scary."

"Not at all. Here's the point. We talked before about building friendship and trust with prospects and clients. This happens when we're sincere and authentic. In fact, these are keys to cultivating a solid relationship with a client."

She chose a sandwich from the tray and then continued. "I don't have to tell you this, but people today are smarter and more informed due to the Internet. Our clients are smarter because they're doing their homework."

"I agree. I know they're much more informed now than even a few years ago when I first started in this business."

"True. That means they can instantly tell if you're just there to make a sale. If you're not sincere about helping them, they'll show you the door.

"I've been around salespeople who are able to 'turn on' their salesman persona. I feel like they're underestimating my intelligence – as though I can't see through that façade."

"Do you find me to be insincere?" Michael didn't want to sound unsure, but he wanted her honest opinion.

"Not at all. Remember, I'm speaking in general terms here. To help us both become more aware. I'm saying that when we're open with our clients and become friends, then we're way ahead in gaining the trust needed to engage as their advisor. All else being equal, your prospect will buy from a friend. All things *not* being equal, your prospect will still buy from a friend."

Vivian reached into her briefcase and pulled out two envelopes along with her smartphone. She held up the first envelope in one hand. "Know what this is? It's an invitation I received to a twenty-fifth anniversary party for a client of mine."

She held up the second envelope in her other hand. "This is a birthday card I plan to send. It's for the daughter of a client; she's going to be eight years old next week. And do you know how I know that?"

Vivian put down the cards and picked up her phone. "A conversation with my prospect is a great opportunity to fact-find, gather personal information, and build up that relationship. When I'm building a relationship with a client, I enter any dates I can find – birthdays, anniversaries, if someone is expecting a baby... Then I follow up by recording the date. Even when their child is about to graduate, I notate it, and one week in advance I offer some acknowledgement – bouquet of flowers, phone call, card, gift, whatever."

Michael was taken aback. He had to admit, he'd never received anything like a bouquet of flowers from any of his clients. Even those he'd maintained for several years.

"Here's a great tip. Clients are more impressed when you remember their kid's birthday than if you remember their own! When you treat a client like a client, you create a boundary. When you treat them like a friend the boundary disappears."

Of course that made sense. "But I always thought I should maintain a business stance with clients. My professional face so to speak."

"Would you do that with one of your buddies?"

"If I did, they'd laugh me all the way into next week."

"Precisely," Vivian said. "Tell me, when a client comes to your office, do you stay behind your desk?"

"Sure. Don't you?"

Vivian shook her head. "I don't. I come around my desk and pull up a chair so we can talk face to face – with no obstruction in between."

She smiled and said, "I can hear your brain working on this one, Michael. You're thinking that it's the proper thing to do with a client. But what I'm saying is, treat your client like a *friend*. Don't be so formal. Formality doesn't build a relationship. How could it?"

"You're right, Vivian. I just never thought about it in those terms."

Vivian told Michael how she often receives referrals from current and past clients. "That's how my business was such a success within a short eight months. When your clients are your friends, they'll trust your advice and follow you for a long time to come."

Michael wondered how much his clients trusted him. At this point he really wasn't sure.

Then Vivian added, "There's a saying in our business: 'It is not what you say or what you did, but how you made them feel' that will make the difference.' No more being a salesperson, Michael. Just be yourself."

Michael knew he had a lot of room for improvement in this area. He planned to do some homework over the weekend and gather more personal information about his clients to better profile and build that important relationship with them.

"As I said before," Vivian told him, "one of the most difficult skills is people skills. They say that to be successful in sales, it's not *what* you know but *who* you know. I disagree. When you build a deep relationship with your clients and referrals starts flowing in, that saying changes to this:

To be successful in sales, it is not what you know – or who you know – it's who knows you."

Michael liked that idea.
Now he had yet one more principle to add to this growing list.

Chapter 13

Lesson 10: Suspect or Prospect

"Having the money and being ready to buy are two different criteria"

One of the side benefits that Michael enjoyed as a result of the past few weeks of coaching with Vivian, was how much more energy he seemed to have. Because his days were productive, he didn't feel the need to work from home in the evenings. (Ellie liked that.) And three days a week, he was back at the gym working out. That too seemed to feed his energy levels.

Basically, his entire outlook on life was changing as his work habits and attitudes changed. He found it to be nothing short of amazing.

Because the weather was growing warmer, Vivian suggested their next Friday meeting be in the open courtyard across from their building. Michael agreed it was a great idea to get out of the stuffy office.

"So," Michael said after they were seated at one of the outdoor tables, "we're all the way to lesson ten. It seems like only yesterday that we were on lesson one."

"A lot has happened in those weeks. I have to commend you on the progress you've made. Every time a new concept is thrown at you, you take it and run with it. You're certainly an easy person to coach."

Michael smiles at the compliment. "You came along at the right time to remind me how much I really want to be a success at this."

"Well, you're certainly on the right track now." Vivian was taking out her laptop and binder.

"So what's on the agenda today?" Michael wanted to know.

"Today, we're going to talk about something that's often very difficult for salespeople."

"Keeping their mouths shut?" Michael asked laughing. It must be the sunshine making him lightheaded.

Vivian laughed right along with him. "Actually that's number *two* on the list of hard-to-do things. No, the first one is learning to walk away from a deal or a client."

"Walk away?" Now that does sound a little foreign."

"There are times when we have to accept the fact that the opportunity to close a sale is not to our benefit. Maybe the client is asking for too much. Maybe they're asking you to shave back your commission. Which, by the way, I never, ever do. When they ask something like that it tells me this person doesn't respect the value of my services."

"I've definitely had that happen to me," Michael said. Then he recounted to her a situation where a client pushed him to not only reduce his commission but also to invest in portfolios that Michael knew would not deliver the results the client wanted in the long run. If he had relented, the client would have been content at the moment, but he would certainly have blamed Michael later when the investment didn't pan out.

"In the end, I did agree to cut my commission slightly, but I was able to convince the client that the investment wasn't in his best interest." Michael frowned at the memory. "Unfortunately, since I cut my commission at that time, the client came back later and expected me to continue reducing my fees. So all in all it was a total loss."

"I don't have to tell you then how important this is."

"I see the point and I agree, but I'm still not sure how you know when and where to draw the line between servicing your client, your company, and yourself?"

Vivian nods thought about that for a moment, then said, "Start by asking yourself if the person is a *prospect* or a *suspect*.

"A prospect is someone who truly wants your help in achieving financial goals. This person respects your knowledge and skills. A suspect, on the other hand, may be someone who only uses your service for that one time. You have to ask yourself if that type of person is worthy of your valuable time and efforts. Better to walk away from a deal than agree to something that is not profitable in the long run, or that won't deliver the required results in the future."

Vivian reminded Michael of what they talked about regarding getting the million-dollar deal. "We're taught to sell to those who have the money. However, just because a person has money, it's not an indication that they're ready and willing to buy from us. They can just as easily be categorized as suspects, and can just as easily waste our time.

"My point here is that we need to focus on the ones who have the money and are ready to *buy* – both. It's just an easier sale and, potentially, you have the chance to upsell them later in the sales process. At the very least, you get your foot in their door!"

Michael knew that Vivian had had more experience with higher net worth clients, and he was now setting his sights on reaching out to that target more aggressively, so this lesson was fascinating to him. "How do you do it?" he asks. "How do you make the right connection and determine where to draw the line?"

"Remember when we spoke about 'making the deal before the deal'?" she replied. "Basically, you're pre-qualifying their desire to move forward. You know they *have* the money, but you need to know if and how they are going to *invest* it. If you don't have the answers to all these questions, you're not in the best position to proceed. Start by asking a few questions, like, 'Do you feel frustrated or disappointed with the low rate of return or the quality of the service you've been getting? Do you feel that it's important for you to make a change in that regard?'

"Now, if the client's reply is not favorable for a potential sale, if the client doesn't reveal a problem for us to help him solve, then this is a suspect, and no longer a prospect."

Vivian went on to share a few stories with Michael about her experiences in walking away from deals. On a few occasions, the clients relented and called her back, agreeing to her recommendations. She said that they usually respect her more for her integrity. Those who don't call back are no big loss. "I just tell myself they're someone else's problem now."

"The best way to find the strength to walk away is by having conviction in what you're trying to achieve. If you truly believe in what you're selling, you sell the solution with all of your heart. If it's so easy to bend, then you really need to strengthen your spine."

Michael was beginning to understand that confidence in his own talents, abilities and knowledge was an underlying factor whether or not he could actually walk away from a prospect who was a time-waster. This was one concept he was anxious to put into practice. He no longer wanted to work with time-wasters; it simply did not fit with his overall plan for success.

Chapter 14

Lesson 11: Invest in Yourself

It was the perfect opportunity for Ellie to meet Vivian. Vivian had invited Michael to one of her Toastmasters' meetings, so Michael told her that both he and Ellie would be there.

When they arrived at a meeting room at the main library, people were already signing in at a table and getting name tags. Vivian saw them and quickly came over, giving them a warm welcome.

After introductions, Ellie told Vivian how much she appreciated all Vivian had done for Michael. "I can see how your coaching has brought back his old enthusiasm," Ellie said, "and it makes a difference in our home life as well."

"It's been my pleasure," Vivian said. "Actually, it's been fun seeing someone like Michael take every concept and run with it."

As Vivian helped get them registered and signed in, Michael noticed that Vivian wore an engraved badge with her name, job title, and their company name. Once again he realized how careful she was to tend to details.

After they were seated, Vivian said to Michael, "I invited you to Toastmasters because I wanted you to see how people use this platform to improve their public speaking. In our business, we need to present ourselves – and our services – with clarity, but also with style and personality. I've been a member now for a little over a year, and I can tell you that my presentation skills have definitely improved."

Michael glanced around at the people in the room. They ranged from college types, to businessmen, to homemakers, to blue collar workers. One distinguished-looking man with greying hair caught Michael's attention.

Vivian saw that Michael had noticed this man. "That's Jimmy," she told him. "He's a young man entering the banking industry. When he was a kid, he has always been extremely shy when speaking in front of a crowd, and he has to do group presentation in his course of work. He joined the club to practise and to overcome his fear. He's been coming here for about six months. He plans to give a presentation to secure an investment portfolio show next month. I wish you could see how he has been transformed by this club!"

Vivian tapped on her tablet and reviewed the notes for her presentation. Suddenly Michael had a moment of panic. "I hope you're not expecting me to get up there and talk tonight!"

Vivian smiled. "Aha! You uncovered my plot!"

"You wouldn't..."

"You're right, I was kidding. No, I invited you here to observe. This is the last of our lessons together and this puts the cap on everything – because it's all about constantly improving yourself and investing in your own growth. I gave you books to read and links to online articles and blogs. Reading is essential, but so is speaking. Toastmasters gives you a safe environment in which to hone your speaking skills."

"Do I need to hone my speaking skills?"

"I don't know. Do you ever make speaking mistakes in front of prospects or clients? Do you get a standing ovation at the end of your presentations?"

Michael stared at Vivian, trying to determine if she was taunting him or speaking seriously. He wondered – *does she get standing ovations?* If anyone could, it would be her.

One by one, members walked to the podium and spent three minutes speaking to the group. When it was Vivian's turn, Michael watched her walk to the front of the room, poised and smiling. She placed her tablet on the podium but looked out at the people in front of her, not the gadget. He and Ellie exchanged glances.

"Hello and welcome everyone," Vivian started out, smiling broadly. Even her eyes were smiling. "I'm Vivian, and I'm so glad you came tonight. I'm going to spend my three minutes talking on the importance of self-growth."

Michael felt like she was speaking directly to him, although her eyes connected with various listeners in the audience. She worked the room beautifully. People were listening, smiling, and nodding their heads in agreement with her statements.

He realized how different she seemed now that he's had time to get to know her. Although she was still young, she possessed more wisdom than many of the more experienced salespeople he knew. Was she one of those "natural-born sellers" who was gifted at birth with these skills? Or did someone teach her in the same way she has taught him?

In the beginning weeks of their coaching sessions, Michael had felt awkward being the student, but that quickly dissipated. Noting her wisdom, he was more than happy to let her take the lead and him follow.

Ellie had grabbed his hand and was holding it tightly. "I'd like to come here too," she whispered to him.

Now that was a good idea. The two of them learning and growing together. Michael smiled over at her.

"Stay curious," Vivian was saying to the audience." Keep learning. Keep asking. You don't need to choose between *get mad* or *get even*. The better choice is to *get better*! Success is a matter of choice. What are *you* going to choose?"

Vivian stepped back from the podium, signalling she was finished. The audience applauded appreciatively. Michael and Ellie were clapping louder than all the others.

Chapter 15

Reap the Rewards

A few weeks after their final lesson, Michael received an email from his boss, Jeff, saying he wanted to see him right away.

He had no idea what that was all about. On his way down the hall to Jeff's office, he stopped to ask Vivian if she knew what was up, but her cubicle was empty. She was probably out on another sales call. Well, no matter about that.

Looking up when Michael appeared at his door, Jeff motioned him in. "Hey there, Michael. Have a chair."

In all Vivian's coaching, she'd never said anything about how avoid feeling nervous when the boss called you in on the carpet.

Jeff was shuffling through a stack of paper on his desk. "I've been looking at your sales activities lately, Michael. I'm seeing a lot of improvement. Can you tell me what's happened here? This is quite a mystery."

Michael stammered a bit. Was it okay to have one of the rookie sales persons become your coach. Would his boss take offense to that? "Well, you see, Jeff, it was Vivian..."

"Vivian? What's Vivian got to do with your sales numbers?" His tone was a little stern.

Now Michael wasn't sure what to say. He wanted to give Vivian full credit for all she'd done for him. "She, well, she just sort of..."

Just then the door flew open and in came Vivian and close behind her was Ellie. They were giggling like two schoolgirls. "Aloha! Aloha, Michael," they were chanting.

They had flower leis in their arms and came over – one of each side of him – and placed the leis around his neck. Ellie leaned over and kissed him on the cheek.

Now Jeff was laughing too. "I know this is a little unconventional, Michael. I usually send a rather impersonal email to let my people know when they've made it into the *Pinnacle Circle of Sales Performers*. But your case is quite unique and quite special. So Vivian here – and your wife as well – asked if we could do this a little differently. And I agreed wholeheartedly."

"You made it," Vivian said. "You're in the Circle."

"And," Ellie added, "we're going to Hawaii." Now she made him stand up so she could hug him. "I'm so proud of you, Michael."

"I have to admit," Jeff said, "I've seen some turnarounds in my career, but I don't remember ever seeing one so dramatic as yours."

He came around his desk and reached out to give Michael a strong handshake. "You deserve every bit of this. And," he added turning to Vivian, "we're considering having this young lady head up some sales training sessions for us."

It had been a very long time since Michael had felt hot tears, but he certainly felt them now. All the hours of hard work were paying off. And now it was time to reap the rewards.

Summary

Congratulations! You have reached the end of this part of your journey. What you do with the eleven lessons in this book is up to you. I hope you will take the time to apply this newfound knowledge to your sales career. Just recognize that change doesn't happen overnight. You must continue to work at sharpening your selling skills every single day. These sales "secrets" will only help you if you apply them steadily enough that they become habit.

1. When you have a strong enough "why," the "how" will follow.
2. When you lose, don't lose the lesson.
3. Pre-qualify your clients before positioning yourself for a potential sale.
4. Master productivity before proficiency.
5. Higher net-worth market you are in, the less competition you will face. If you think small, you risk staying in that mindset.
6. Emulate yourself after someone you aspire to be like, is the way to accelerate your success. First mirror others, then you can become an original.
7. Harness the power of persuasion, you must learn to ask the right questions, tell a story about your solution, convert your weaknesses into strengths, and always stay in control of your presentation.
8. Your job is to understand your clients' problems and sell the problem to them. Leave the educating to the teachers. Once the prospect

realizes he has a problem, then your proposed solution is just a process of implementation.

9. Be a friend first and a salesperson second.

10. Know when you need to walk away from a deal or a client.

11. Self-improvement is not a finite task. Keep challenging yourself to be and do better.

I encourage you to come back to this book from time to time and revisit Michael's story. Consider how each lesson applies to you, your clients, and your methods. Strive to do better and continue to learn and grow, as a sales professional and a person.

There is tremendous satisfaction in empowering others, whether you do so as a manager, colleague, or trainer. So I also hope that you will pass these secrets along to your colleagues and trainees.

I've spent the last twelve years in sales, and I plan to continue for a long time to come. I hope the lessons in this book will help you to launch yourself toward a more rewarding career.

There is no secret to success, no magic formula. You have the power to be whoever you want to be.

Good luck!

—Kevin Foo

Second Title Coming Soon
Watch for our next book coming out soon entitled:

"From No to No Problem!"
This book focuses on helping sales people overcome objections with proven and practical methods that they can immediately use.

Printed in the United States
By Bookmasters